Penguins

Penguins

A Carolrhoda Nature Watch Book

written and photographed by Lynn M. Stone

Carolrhoda Books, Inc. / Minneapolis

For my mom and dad, who first opened for me the windows to the great outdoors, and for my wife and daughter, who encourage the naturalist in me.

The publisher wishes to thank Gerald Kooyman, Ph.D., Research Professor at Scripps Institution of Oceanography, for his time and expertise.

Text copyright © 2003 by Lynn M. Stone
Photographs copyright © 2003 by Lynn M. Stone, except as noted on page 48

Carolrhoda Books, Inc.
A division of Lerner Publishing Group
241 First Avenue North
Minneapolis, MN 55401 U.S.A.

Website address: www.lernerbooks.com

Library of Congress Cataloging-in-Publication Data

Stone, Lynn M.
    Penguins / written and photographed by Lynn M. Stone.
      p.   cm. — (A Carolrhoda nature watch book)
    Summary: Describes the physical characteristics, behavior, and habitat of penguins.
    ISBN: 0–87614–907–7 (lib. bdg. : alk. paper)
    1. Penguins—Juvenile literature. [1. Penguins.] I. Title. II. Series.
    QL696.S473 S75 2003
    598.47—dc21   2001006589

Manufactured in the United States of America
1 2 3 4 5 6 – JR – 08 07 06 05 04 03

CONTENTS

Penguins walk on short legs, holding their wings out for balance.

With its smooth white front and black back, you could almost imagine that this penguin is wearing a tuxedo.

UNUSUAL BIRDS

They can't fly. They swim smoothly through cold seas. On land, they walk upright on stubby legs. Their sleek feathers are black and white, and some people say they look like well-dressed waiters. What are these creatures?

Don't be fooled. They're penguins, not fish, seals, or little people. Despite their unusual features, penguins are birds. Just like ravens and robins and magpies and macaws, penguins have feathers and beaks, lay eggs, and are warm blooded.

But penguins are remarkable birds. They're **seabirds,** meaning that they spend most of their lives in the water. Instead of using their wings to fly, they use them as flippers when they swim and dive. Some of penguins' most amazing feats involve diving. Some kinds of penguins dive longer and deeper than almost any other bird.

Penguins do not spend all their time at sea. They have to come ashore at certain times of the year to rest, mate, and raise young. Since penguins get their food from the ocean, there's nothing for them to eat on land. Many penguins have to fast, or go without food. Penguins can fast for longer periods of time than any other bird. Some penguins survive for not only days, but for months, without a meal. The males of one kind of penguin may go for as long as 4 months without eating!

Not impressed? Consider that some penguins live on and around the continent of Antarctica, the most frigid place on the planet. They live and nest farther south than any other kind of bird. From deep diving to fasting to braving cold weather, penguins are truly unusual birds. But that's just the beginning of their remarkable story.

Some penguins make their homes on the rocky shores of Antarctica, the southernmost continent.

These penguins nest with a bird relative, the black-browed albatross, in the Falkland Islands.

THE PENGUIN FAMILY

Ornithologists (or-nih-THAH-luh-jihsts) are scientists who study birds. They place birds into groups according to certain features, such as the shape of a bird's skeleton or beak.

According to ornithologists, penguins' closest relatives are some of the other seabirds. Penguins are related to petrels, albatrosses, and frigate birds. Unlike penguins, some of these birds are among the most accomplished flying birds in the world.

All penguins belong to a scientific group called a **family.** The penguin family is called Spheniscidae. The penguin family's special features include black and white, scale-like feathers and thin wings that don't enable them to fly but are perfect for swimming. Penguins walk upright on their short legs and flat, webbed feet.

Within the penguin family, ornithologists have identified six smaller groups. Each **genus** is made up of kinds of penguins that are closely related to one another. In all, there are 17 **species,** or kinds, of penguins. Penguins of the same species can mate and produce young. They share the same general size, body structure, behavior, and coloring. They also share the same **habitat,** or the environment in which an animal lives.

The two largest species of penguins, the king and the emperor, belong to the genus known as *Aptenodytes.* These penguins have similar **plumage,** or feathers. Both king and emperor penguins have orange or yellow patches of feathers on the sides of their heads and on their chests.

Three species of penguins make up the genus called *Pygoscelis.* These penguins, the gentoo, Adélie (ah-DAY-lee), and chinstrap, are often called brush-tailed penguins because they have stiff tail feathers.

The king is the second largest penguin species. It stands about 33 inches (85 cm) tall.

A third genus, *Eudyptes,* includes six kinds of penguins that have showy crests of feathers on their heads. The crested penguins are the rockhopper, fiordland, Snares, erect-crested, macaroni, and royal penguins.

A fourth genus, *Spheniscus,* includes the four species of banded penguins—the magellanic, African, Humboldt, and Galápagos. Penguins in these species have black bands on their chests.

Top: *The magellanic penguin got its name from Portuguese explorer Ferdinand Magellan. It is the largest of the banded penguins.*
Middle: *A rockhopper penguin perches on a rock, ready to take a leap.*
Bottom: *Can you tell how the chinstrap penguin got its name?*

11

The yellow-eyed penguin, which has yellow bands around its eyes and head, is the only species in its genus, *Megadyptes*. The little penguin, sometimes called the blue penguin or the little blue penguin, is also the only species in its genus, *Eudyptula*. Its back is gray blue, while its front is white.

Most penguins have brown or red eyes, but the yellow-eyed penguin (top) *has yellow eyes. The little penguin* (bottom) *stands about 16 inches (40 cm) tall.*

Even though all the penguin species are in the same family, they vary greatly in appearance. Think about just their difference in size. Some emperor penguins stand more than 3 feet (90 cm) tall and weigh up to 90 pounds (40 kg). King penguins are almost the same height, but they weigh closer to 26 pounds (12 kg). In contrast to these heavyweights, the smallest penguin, the little, weighs barely 2 pounds (1 kg)! The other penguin species weigh between 6 and 17 pounds (3–8 kg).

The 17 penguin species also differ widely in their **ranges,** or living areas. Most people picture penguins among towers of ice, somewhere in or near Antarctica, the frozen continent where the South Pole lies. That image is accurate only to a point.

Maximum Sizes* of Selected Penguin Species

INCHES

Emperor
51 in. (130 cm)

Gentoo
35 in. (90 cm)

Yellow-eyed
31 in. (78 cm)

Magellanic
28 in. (70 cm)

Rockhopper
23 in. (58 cm)

Little
18 in. (45 cm)

*Measurements are made from tip of beak to tip of tail.

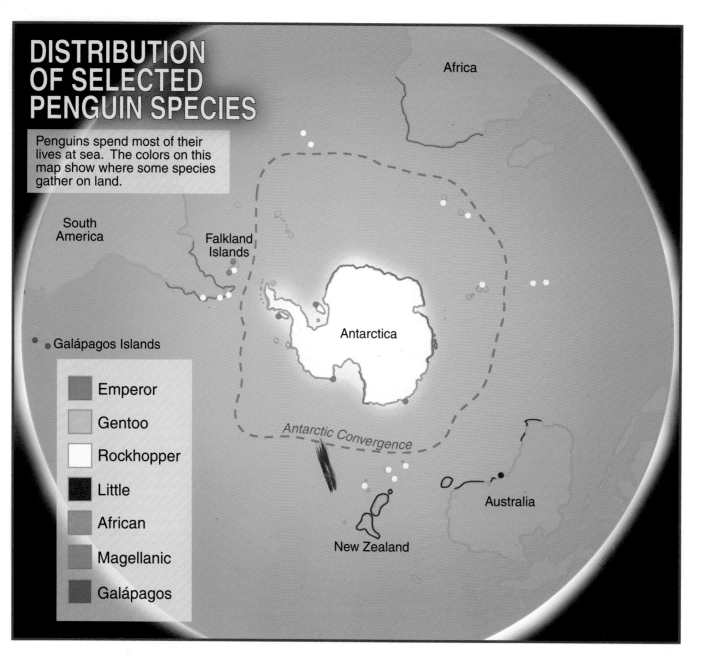

DISTRIBUTION OF SELECTED PENGUIN SPECIES

Penguins spend most of their lives at sea. The colors on this map show where some species gather on land.

Africa

South America

Falkland Islands

Galápagos Islands

Antarctica

Antarctic Convergence

New Zealand

Australia

Emperor

Gentoo

Rockhopper

Little

African

Magellanic

Galápagos

Only four species of penguins, the emperor, the Adélie, the gentoo, and the chinstrap, live in Antarctica. The other species live in other parts of the Southern Hemisphere, the lands and seas south of the equator. North of Antarctica are such places as New Zealand, Australia, and the southern coasts of South America and Africa. Penguins live in all these places, some of which have warm weather!

In sheer numbers of birds, most penguins live in an area north of Antarctica, but south of a line that scientists call the Antarctic Convergence. *Convergence* means "bringing together." At the Antarctic Convergence, northern ocean water meets the colder, food-rich southern ocean water. Within this great marine world, south of the convergence and north of Antarctica, are dozens of islands, large and small, where penguins raise their young.

The greatest number of penguin species live north of that region. Seven species live on the mainland of southern New Zealand and on its offshore islands.

Five species of penguins live around the Falkland Islands, which lie off the southern shores of Argentina. Some species, such as the gentoo and king, live both north and south of the Antarctic Convergence.

The Galápagos penguin may have the most surprising habitat. It lives only on Fernandina and Isabela, large islands in the Galápagos chain. The Galápagos Islands, famous for their giant tortoises and other unusual wildlife, lie near the equator. The climate on the islands is warm, sunny, and tropical. But the ocean water around Fernandina and Isabela is cold, like the chilled seas where other penguins feed.

Galápagos penguins keep cool by heading to the ocean on hot days. They come ashore at night, when the air is cooler.

This chinstrap penguin spreads its wings, but not to fly. Its wings are too small.

BUILT FOR SEA AND LAND

Why don't penguins fly? The answer lies in the way penguins **evolved,** or changed slowly over thousands of years. Birds generally fly to find food, to avoid danger, and to reach safe places for building nests and raising their young. But as ancient penguins evolved, they filled niches, or special roles in their habitat, where none of these reasons applied.

As seabirds, penguins find their food by swimming and diving, rather than flying. Their cold, isolated homes in Antarctica and other distant places have few dangerous animals to avoid. And most penguins nest near the seashore, so they don't need to fly to raise their young. As a result of these circumstances, penguins evolved into flightless birds.

Since penguins are frequent swimmers, it's no surprise that they evolved strong abilities in this area. Penguins have several **adaptations,** or special features that help animals live in their environment, for living in water, especially cold water.

Penguins' bodies are shaped so that they can easily move through cold seas. A penguin has a long body and feet set well back toward its tail. This torpedo-like shape is ideal for undersea swimming. A torpedo glides through the water more easily than, for instance, an ostrich of the same weight. That's because the streamlined torpedo shape has less drag, or resistance to water.

Another adaptation that allows penguins to get around well in the sea is their bone structure. Penguin bones are heavy and solid. Most birds have bones that are filled with air. Light, hollow bones help keep a bird's weight low, allowing it to fly more easily. But solid bones are useful to penguins. They help a penguin sink and dive more easily, so it uses less energy in moving underwater.

Penguins' wings help them swim and dive, too. Flat and narrow, covered by short, stiff feathers, penguin wings are useless for flight in the air. But they're strong, effective flippers, and they propel a penguin in what ornithologists sometimes call "underwater flight."

Propelling itself with strong wings, a Galápagos penguin seems to fly through the water.

and brighter than the surrounding water. A white-bellied animal would probably be hard to see from below. When an animal near the surface looks down toward darker water, the dark back of another animal would be hard to see. So a penguin's coloring may help it escape the notice of both its enemies and the sea animals it hunts.

Like most penguins, this Adélie penguin has a black back (above left) *and a white front* (above)*.*

The black and white coloring of penguins may be an adaptation to the ocean environment. Like many other sea animals, such as killer whales, adult penguins have dark coloring on their back and light coloring on their front. Some scientists think that such a color scheme makes an animal less visible at sea. When an animal swimming below the surface looks up, the water above appears lighter

18

Penguins' feathers help the birds survive in cold environments. A penguin must keep cold water and cold air away from its skin, so thick, waterproof, and clean feathers are essential. Short, stiff penguin feathers are knit into a dense blanket of insulation. They keep heat in and cold air and water out.

Penguins clean and waterproof their feathers with their beaks in an activity called **preening.** Like other seabirds, a penguin produces natural oils, some of which are stored in the uropygial (yur-uh-PIE-jee-uhl), or preen, gland at the base of its tail. The penguin dips its beak in the oil and applies it to its feathers. The oil coats the feathers, waterproofing them and stopping the growth of fungi and bacteria.

While many polar animals depend on blubber, or fat, for insulation, most penguins depend far more on feathers. The emperor penguin, however, has a fairly thick layer of blubber in addition to its cloak of feathers at some times of the year. In its Antarctic habitat, air temperatures reach −40°F (−40°C) and seawater temperatures reach 29°F (−2°C). The emperor penguin needs both feathers and fat to stay warm.

Penguins' bodies have other adaptations to cold. Some of their body parts—the feet, wings, and head—don't have thick feathers but are exposed to cold air. Penguins that live in cold places can lose heat through those areas. They have smaller feet, flippers, and beaks than penguins that live in warmer climates. In addition, the blood vessels in the exposed parts are arranged to limit the amount of lost heat. This way, penguins can stay warm in cold temperatures.

A king penguin applies oil to the feathers on its wings.

19

When walking isn't fast enough, penguins toboggan down snowy hills (above). *On the way up, penguins sometimes use their beaks to help them climb* (right).

Penguins also have adaptations to help them survive on land. Penguins get around fairly well on land. They are able to hike along narrow paths that snake through snow or wild grasses. Some of those paths are long, slippery, and steep. High-climbing penguins sometimes use their beaks like pickaxes to help raise themselves up steep hills. If they need to descend snowy slopes quickly, penguins will toboggan—slide on their bellies and propel themselves with their legs—down snowy slopes. And rockhopper penguins are accomplished at—what else?—leaping from rock to rock.

FINDING FOOD

Ornithologists know more about penguins' lives on land than their lives at sea. Penguins are easier to study on land than in the deep, cold ocean water where they swim and hunt. But ornithologists know some things about penguins' underwater habits, including how the birds find food.

Ornithologists know, for example, that penguins are **predators,** or animals that hunt and eat other animals. Penguins catch vast numbers of the smaller animals that make up their **prey,** animals they hunt and eat. The world's penguins eat about 20 million tons of seafood—small fish, squid, and shrimplike animals called krill—per year.

A penguin's diet depends on its species. Emperor and king penguins eat mostly fish. Other penguins, including gentoos, Adélies, chinstraps, and the crested penguins, live on krill. Most penguins mix squid into their diet.

A krill

Diving in and out of the water, a penguin porpoises out to sea. It swims like the whales that are called porpoises.

A penguin on the way to sea to hunt must try to avoid being hunted itself. To quickly reach open water, where their predators do not travel, the penguin swims by **porpoising.** It leaps briefly from the sea to breathe and then goes back into the water, much like a flying fish. Porpoising speed averages almost 7 miles per hour (10 km/h).

When a penguin is farther from shore and doesn't fear attack, it makes shallow travel dives. These dives take it about 3 feet (1 m) beneath the surface of the water. Its swimming speed averages about 4.5 miles per hour (7.2 km/h).

Most penguin prey swims well below the water's surface, so a penguin must dive deep to find and catch it. Penguin prey travels in schools, or swarms, so a penguin can catch and eat several prey animals in a single dive. It takes many gulps during each dive to grab its prey.

Since a penguin swallows a little seawater along with its prey, it takes in salt at the same time. Penguins have large salt glands that help them avoid salt overload. Salt glands are located over the penguin's eyes, above the base of the beak. The glands filter excess salt from the blood and release it through the bird's nostrils.

How deep do penguins dive, and for how long? To find out, scientists have fitted wild penguins with electronic devices that record this information. These devices have shown that medium-sized penguins can dive 300 feet (90 m) below the surface of the ocean. Emperors dive deeper than other penguins, up to at least 1,755 feet (535 m), or about one-third of a mile. They not only dive deeper than other penguins, they stay underwater longer. The longest known penguin dive was a 22-minute plunge by an emperor. Medium-sized penguins typically dive for 30 seconds to 1 minute.

In order to dive for such long periods, penguins must store enough oxygen in their blood and muscles to survive undersea for several minutes. Oxygen is stored mainly in hemoglobin, a substance in the blood, and in myoglobin in the birds' muscles. Penguins have unusually high amounts of myoglobin, which suggests at least one way they store oxygen for dives.

After a penguin has eaten its fill, it returns to land. In most cases, it has traveled between 10 and 50 miles (16–80 km). King penguins sometimes log hunting trips of up to 375 miles (600 km). These trips can last up to three months.

Bellies full after a hunting trip, penguins return to land.

A macaroni penguin colony

LIFE IN PENGUIN COLONIES

Imagine that you could follow returning penguins from the sea onto land. You would see one of nature's spectacular views. Thousands upon thousands of birds cover the ground for almost as far as you can see. Penguins stretch from the beach inland, like a broad, living blanket of birds.

Up close, you see that the area hums with activity. Penguins feed their young and defend their nests. They come and go in little groups, some heading toward the sea, others returning to land. The air is smelly from the penguins' seafood diet. You hear loud penguin croaks, squawks, and trumpet calls. Mud, feathers, and guano—the penguins' droppings—litter the ground.

This is a penguin **colony.** All penguins leave the sea to form pairs, mate, build nests, lay eggs, raise young, and **molt,** or grow new feathers to replace old ones. Most penguin species carry out these activities in colonies. They come to land and lay eggs in the late spring, and then raise their chicks during the summer. (Summer in the Southern Hemisphere takes place during the northern winter, roughly December through February.)

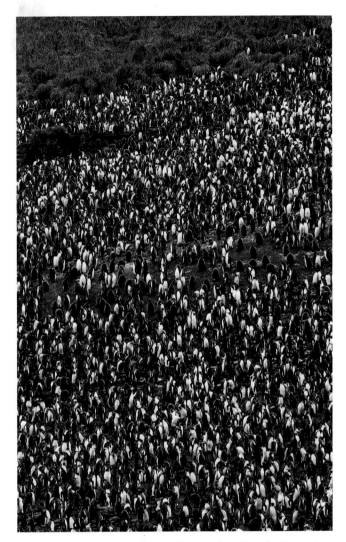

King penguins crowd together in this South Georgia Island colony.

Although most penguin species gather in these large, densely populated groups, two species do not. Fiordland and yellow-eyed penguins build their nests alone or in small groups.

Many penguin colonies have hundreds or thousands of members. One Adélie colony is home to more than 200,000 birds! The colonies turn entire slopes and plains into black and white penguin factories. Some colonies have fewer than 100 pairs, especially gentoo colonies.

Penguins stick with so many others of their kind for several reasons. One reason is limited nesting habitat. Penguins need to build their nests in a site that has fairly good access to the sea so that they can easily hunt for food. Also, colonies probably offer some protection from some kinds of predators. With so many birds packed together, predators can't possibly kill them all. Furthermore, once eggs are laid and hatched, the presence of large numbers of adult birds acts as a defense for the young.

Tens of thousands of king penguins live in this colony on South Georgia Island. Many other seabirds, such as herons, geese, and cormorants, also live in colonies.

Emperor penguins rest on an ice floe near Antarctica.

Penguin colonies are found in a variety of habitats. Most penguin species make their colonies on land. Kings choose flat, open areas beneath coastal cliffs or gently sloping hills. Other species gather among tufts of grass. Galápagos penguins live in the cracks of their islands' moonscape of lava rock. The banded penguins often live in a honeycomb of burrows near the seashore. Others, such as macaronis and chinstraps, may hike up steep, rocky slopes up to 1,650 feet (500 m) above the sea.

Emperors are the only penguins that don't come to land to make their colonies. Their colonies are on firm ice that extends like a shelf from the mainland shore of Antarctica. Unless an emperor strays northward on a floating iceberg, as sometimes happens, it will never see plants growing in earth! Emperors are the only birds in the world that don't need to visit real land during their lifetime, which may exceed 20 years.

Most colonies are within several hundred yards of the shore. But there are exceptions. Some gentoo and king penguin colonies are up to 2 miles (3 km) inland. Emperors make an even longer journey. They sometimes hike 30 to 75 miles (50–120 km) across the firm sea ice to their colonies.

After penguins arrive at their colonies, males of most species claim sites to build nests. Then adult males and females get ready to court, or form pairs. Each penguin takes one mate for a nesting, or breeding, season. Many penguins take the same mate during future nesting seasons. Pairs of kings and emperors are less likely to stay together during more than one season.

During courtship, penguins engage in several body postures or movements called displays. The behaviors differ somewhat from one species to another. In many species, males swing their heads and trumpet loudly. Such behavior signals that a male has claimed a nest site and is looking for a mate. After a female has joined the male at the nest site, the two penguins perform another display. Both partners may trumpet, bow, and perform other movements.

Kings and emperors perform one of the most dramatic displays. The male and female stand very tall with beaks pointing upward. Then they lower their beaks and waddle through the colony. Like many other displays, this one seems to help a penguin pair form.

Hoping to attract a mate to his nesting site, a male king penguin trumpets.

28

Once a pair has formed, the penguins mate. Then most penguins turn their energy toward building nests. Penguin nests are a mixed lot. Ground nests of penguins are generally shallow scrapes in the ground lined with grass, a few feathers, and perhaps twigs, moss, or old bones. Several species, including gentoos, Adélies, and chinstraps, often nest on little bowls of pebbles. The penguins collect the pebbles in their beaks and place them in the nests. One medium-sized gentoo nest contained 1,700 stones. The stone counter must have had as much patience as the nest builder!

Pebbles are useful materials for nests in places where plants don't grow. A pebble nest built a few inches above the ground can save eggs or chicks (baby penguins) from drowning if flooding occurs.

Above: *A gentoo carries a pebble to its nest.*
Left: *This macaroni penguin's nest is made of dried grasses.*

29

Species such as the Humboldt and magellanic penguins use their feet to dig burrows in soft soil. Little penguins are diggers, too, but they also borrow the empty burrows of another seabird, the short-tailed shearwater.

Nesting penguins are always on guard. They defend their patches of ground from other penguins by pecking, biting, grasping each other's beaks, and striking with their wings. In crowded colonies, a penguin guarding a nest is likely to jab at any penguin that passes close by, whatever the passerby's intention.

Above left: *A gentoo penguin scolds a potential pebble thief.*
Above: *A magellanic penguin peers out of its burrow nest. The burrow provides protection from the wind and sun.*

When the nest is done, the female penguin is ready to lay her eggs. She lays eggs when the days are long, food is plentiful, and the weather is fairly stable. The females of most penguin species normally lay two eggs each. King and emperor penguins lay just one egg.

Eggs must be **incubated,** or kept warm by the parents, until the eggs hatch. Except for emperors, both male and female penguins share the incubation duties. Incubation takes from 1 to 2 months, depending on the species.

During nesting season, penguin parents develop a **brood patch,** a small, nearly featherless area on their breast. They incubate their eggs by pressing the brood patch against them. A penguin's skin is warmer than its outer layer of feathers. By keeping the brood patch against the egg, an adult penguin transfers plenty of heat.

Perched on its pebble nest, a gentoo incubates its eggs. Can you spot the penguin's brood patch?

Kings and emperors care for their eggs in a most unusual way. They incubate their eggs by holding them on the top of their feet with the help of a special flap of belly skin. Kings make shallow ground nests, but emperors don't have nests at all.

Male emperors incubate their eggs while females are feeding at sea. The males manage to hold the egg on their feet for more than 2 months. And they do it during the dark Antarctic winter, beginning in late May.

The male emperors don't eat during this time—they live without food for up to 115 days during the period of courtship and the incubation of their eggs. The average air temperature is −4°F (−20°C), and the wind may howl in hurricane gusts. To stay warm, the males squeeze together in large, dense groups called huddles. Still holding the eggs on their feet, birds rotate from outside to inside. Sooner or later, all the individuals share the community heat.

A king penguin checks on its egg. Kings keep their eggs warm by holding them against a bare patch of skin on their belly.

RAISING PENGUIN CHICKS

While penguin parents incubate their eggs, a chick develops inside each egg. After incubation, the chicks break out of their eggs with the help of a small, hard knob on their upper beak, called an egg tooth. Among the smaller species, hatching can take 1 full day. An emperor or king penguin chick may take up to 3 days to hatch.

Some birds, such as geese and ducks, leave their nests almost immediately after hatching and feed themselves, although they remain in the company of parents.

Penguin chicks, however, are helpless when they hatch. They depend on adult penguins for food and warmth.

Penguin chicks are covered by a thin coat of soft, fluffy feathers called down, but that's not enough insulation to keep them from freezing. So adult penguins keep the chicks warm. They tuck the chicks under their bodies, against their brood patch. **Brooding** maintains a chick's body temperature and protects the chick from storms and predators.

After 35 days of incubation, this chinstrap egg is hatching.

Tucked under its mother's belly flap, an emperor chick stays safe and warm.

Most penguin couples share brooding duties. But among the six crested penguin species, males do all the brooding. Female emperors brood their chicks with their feet and belly flaps while the males, who have been the sole incubators, return to the sea to feed.

Most penguins brood their young for between 2 and 6 weeks. Brooding gradually ends as a chick grows and develops a thicker covering of down. By this time, chicks are too large to squeeze against the brood patch.

Penguin chicks depend on their parents for food. Since penguins live strictly on seafood, whatever a young penguin eats must be brought to it from the sea by a parent. The only way a penguin can ship seafood from ocean to land is in its belly.

As adults return to their nests, they regurgitate, or vomit, a partly digested seafood stew for their chicks. The chicks peck at it. Later, when the chicks grow older and stronger, they dip their beaks into the parents' mouths for food.

Most penguin chicks have their first meal within a day or two of hatching. But macaroni, rockhopper, and some Adélie chicks aren't fed for up to 1 week after hatching. These youngsters live on the yolk reserves their bodies have absorbed from the egg. The yolk contains fats, which are a source of energy.

The situation is different with emperors. By the time an emperor chick hatches, its father, who has been incubating the egg, has fasted for up to 16 weeks. The female emperors have been feeding at sea. They are due back to the colony any day with food for the chicks. Meanwhile, the male emperor regurgitates a protein-rich paste for his chick to eat.

As penguin chicks grow, they spend more time together and less time with their parents. The chicks of most species form groups called **crèches** (KRESH-uhz). A crèche may have a few penguins or several hundred. Like the colony as a whole, the crèche provides some protection from weather and predators.

With their chick in a crèche, both penguin parents leave the colony to feed at sea. They return daily or every few days to feed their chicks.

This 11-month-old king chick still relies on a parent for food. It reaches into its parent's mouth for some regurgitated krill.

Before they fledge, king penguin chicks are covered with brown, fluffy feathers.

In the crèche stage, penguins change dramatically, from downy chicks to full-feathered penguins. The length of time it takes to **fledge,** or develop adult plumage, depends upon the species and the availability of food. Some species take from 7 to 11 weeks to fledge. Gentoo and yellow-eyed penguins take about 3.5 months. Emperors take 5 months to fledge. Kings take from 10 to 13 months.

As chicks near fledging, they spend more time at the edge of the water. They may briefly bob in the surf, but they soon waddle back to the shore. Eventually, all young penguins paddle awkwardly into the sea as young adults. Instinctively, they dive and catch their own food. At this point in their lives, almost all of them are totally independent of their parents.

Fledging in itself does not make a penguin an adult. A young penguin doesn't have the same dark, shiny plumage as its parents. Its feathers are grey and dull instead. It won't be ready to begin its own family the next nesting season. Most penguins do not begin mating until they are at least 2 years old. Emperors are usually 5 years old before they are ready to mate.

How soon a young penguin returns to land after going to sea depends on its species. Most penguin species are **migratory.** Like many other wild birds, they travel great distances at certain times of the year, normally in spring and fall. Ornithologists aren't yet certain where penguins travel. But they do know that the newly fledged youngsters of most migratory penguin species usually don't return to the colony until the next nesting season. The chicks of nonmigratory, or resident, penguins, such as the Galápagos, return to the colony regularly after feeding trips.

While young penguins swim out to sea, adults of nearly all penguin species molt. The birds don't lose all of their feathers at once. As new feathers grow into place, the old, worn feathers fall away. Molting can be a lengthy process for most birds, but penguins renew their plumage in just 2 to 4 weeks.

Because they can't stay warm in the water without all of their feathers, penguins must remain on shore while they molt. This forces them to fast. But before they molt, penguins go to sea to fatten up, increasing their weight by more than half. After the molt, covered with new feathers, penguins return to sea to hunt. The migratory species probably remain at sea during the winter, roughly from April or May through September or October. The resident species return to their colonies and other land sites throughout the winter.

A molting king penguin

PENGUINS AT RISK

Penguins have survived, even prospered, without being able to fly because they have few natural enemies. But like most animals, even penguins become prey at times. One predator of penguins is the leopard seal. In certain locations, leopard seals grab penguins when they enter or exit the sea. Fur seals, southern sea lions, sharks, and toothed whales also occasionally attack penguins at sea.

On land, adult penguins are usually safe from predators. If you're wondering about polar bears, they're at the opposite end of the globe, in the Arctic—some 10,000 miles (16,000 km) away from most penguin colonies.

Most predators that raid penguin colonies are after unguarded eggs or chicks. In Australia and the Galápagos Islands, snakes sometimes steal penguin eggs. But in Antarctica and on nearby islands, the most common and widespread predator of penguins ashore is another bird—the skua, a large, gull-like bird. In some colonies, skuas feed on dead or dying chicks or penguin eggs.

Leopard seals (above left) **wait to attack penguins beneath the surface of the water. Others wait for careless penguins on ice floes. A skua** (above right) **often surprises a nesting penguin by sneaking up on it. The skua pulls the penguin's tail feathers to distract it from its egg or chick.**

Left: *A sheathbill will sometimes fly at an adult penguin, startling it into regurgitating its food.*
Above: *These king penguins don't seem to notice an elephant seal.*

Several other birds are predators of penguins. The giant petrel preys on chicks. The sheathbill is a much smaller bird than either the skua or the giant petrel, and it isn't big enough to threaten chicks. Instead, sheathbills gobble unguarded eggs. In northern penguin colonies, gulls are predators of penguin eggs and chicks.

Penguins share beaches with many kinds of seals. Seals, like penguins, come ashore to raise families. Some of them, such as elephant seals, don't eat penguins. In fact, penguins often hop onto sleepy elephant seals as if they were overstuffed beach toys. But fights between the huge seals, which weigh up to 8,000 pounds (3,600 kg), can result in penguins being squashed. Fighting male elephant seals have occasionally destroyed penguins by bulldozing through their colonies.

A significant threat to penguins comes from humans. The first recorded human contact with penguins was probably in 1497, during Portuguese explorer Vasco da Gama's voyage to India. In the centuries since, people have often used penguins for their own gain. In the 1800s and early 1900s, for example, seal hunters and sailors killed huge numbers of penguins, mostly kings. They were slaughtered mainly for their blubber, which could be boiled into oil. Penguin meat was salted and dried and used for food. Their skins were sometimes used to make trim for fashionable caps, purses, slippers, and clothes.

Traditionally, penguin eggs have been more valuable than the birds themselves. Sailors and local settlers once collected huge numbers of eggs for food. In 1897 alone, more than 700,000 eggs were taken from African penguin colonies. Until the 1970s, about 10,000 gentoo eggs were taken from colonies in the Falkland Islands each year. Egging continues, but it is no longer common.

As recently as the early 1980s, a Japanese company requested permission to harvest penguins in Argentina. The plan was to use the birds for oil, meat, and skins. The skins would have been made into golf gloves. Argentina did not approve the plan.

Killing penguins was never difficult for humans. Unfamiliar with large predators on land, penguins reacted to their human enemies with curiosity rather than fear. The reception is the same today when boatloads of visitors step ashore to visit penguin colonies. Penguins usually treat humans with barely a second glance. Sometimes, in their stately but clumsy way, the birds actually approach the people.

Even when humans aren't hunting penguins, their actions affect the birds. Penguin colonies are usually on remote islands where wild mammals don't exist. But over the last 200 years, people have introduced mammals such as cats, dogs, weasels, ferrets, and rats to areas near penguin colonies. Some of the mammals escaped from the ships of whale and seal hunters. Others were introduced to control other native wildlife that the human residents considered to be pests. Especially on islands with warmer climates, these mammals can survive winters and multiply, eating penguins and other birds that nest on the ground.

These macaroni penguins on South Georgia Island ignore the tourists taking their pictures.

The population of fiordland penguins in New Zealand has been threatened by rats, which eat eggs and kill adults and chicks. The rats came from ships visiting New Zealand shores. The population of fiordland penguins may number fewer than 1,000 pairs. In South America, the population of Humboldt penguins is less than 20,000.

Pollution from ships is also harmful to penguins. When ships carrying oil leak or spill oil into the ocean, penguins—and their food supply—get sick or die. Scientists think that 40,000 magellanic penguins die each year as a result of oil pollution. An oil spill near South Africa killed almost 2,000 African penguins in the year 2000.

Human activities have caused some penguin species to become **endangered,** or at risk of dying out. For example, New Zealand's yellow-eyed penguins are endangered on the country's mainland and rare on the islands where they nest. Their population is around 5,000.

Laws aren't always enforced, but penguins are generally protected by the laws of the nations in which they live. And in Antarctica, which is owned by no nation, a treaty among several countries protects penguins and other wildlife. The population of penguins in Antarctica is healthy. Most colonies are either stable or growing. Still, in the years ahead, penguins everywhere may face serious problems that result from **global warming,** an increase of the earth's temperature.

The population of yellow-eyed penguins was larger before European settlers arrived in New Zealand.

Penguins catch a ride on a drifting iceberg near Antarctica.

Global warming is the result of a buildup in the earth's atmosphere of certain gases. The gases are by-products from the burning of fossil fuels such as gasoline and coal. Most scientists believe that these pollutants are gradually raising the earth's average temperatures.

The problem for penguins is that any long-term climate change is likely to change the temperatures of ocean currents. That change would, in turn, alter the populations of the prey that penguins eat. Penguins might not be able to find food. Certain prey species might thrive in a warmer or cooler ocean, while others might not.

43

Left: *If the ocean's temperature rises, ice may melt, causing sea levels to rise. Penguin colonies could be flooded.*
Right: *The future of penguins depends on how humans take care of the environment.*

The same is true of penguins. Some species might benefit from changes in the ocean's temperature, but others are likely to be victims of those changes. Climate change would also change the land habitats of penguins. Penguins might not be able to find new places to form colonies. Changes to temperatures on land and in the water may make it hard for penguins to survive.

Fortunately, the world has not ignored the problem of global warming. Nations are wrestling with ways to better control the release of pollutants into the atmosphere. In the United States, for example, the government sets limits on the amounts of pollutants that a factory or vehicle can discharge into the atmosphere. However, U.S. standards will have to be tightened, just as they will elsewhere, if the world wants to combat global warming successfully. One positive sign is that scientists continue to develop uses of different fuel sources, such as solar energy, to eliminate some uses of fossil fuels altogether.

We know that polar bears aren't a problem at all for penguins. Gulls, skuas, leopard seals, and even the tiger snakes that nab a penguin once in a while on Australian shores aren't big problems. The real problem in the penguins' future is how we treat the world in which they live.

GLOSSARY

adaptations: changes that enable a plant or animal to survive in a specific environment

brood: to keep chicks or eggs warm by holding them against the brood patch

brood patch: a featherless area of skin that birds use to warm their eggs and young

colony: a nesting area where birds of the same species form pairs and raise their young

crèche: a group of young penguins that stay together for warmth and protection

endangered: at risk of dying out forever

evolve: to change slowly over thousands of years

family: a scientific group of plants or animals with many features in common. It usually includes more than one genus, or subgroup.

fledge: to grow adult feathers

genus: a group of several related kinds of plants or animals

global warming: the gradual increase of the earth's temperature

habitat: the type of environment in which an animal or plant normally lives

incubate: to keep an egg warm and care for it until it hatches

migratory: traveling to a new area at certain times of the year

molt: to lose old feathers and replace them with new ones

ornithologists: scientists who study birds

plumage: all the feathers on a bird

porpoise: to dive in and out of the water. The porpoise, an ocean animal, swims like this.

predators: animals that hunt, kill, and eat other animals

preen: to clean and waterproof feathers

prey: animals that are hunted and eaten by other animals

range: the area in which a type of plant or animal lives

seabird: a type of bird that lives most of its life in the ocean

species: a kind of plant or animal. Members of the same species have common traits. They can mate and produce young that are like themselves.

INDEX

ABOUT THE AUTHOR

Author and photographer **Lynn M. Stone** has written more than 400 books and has traveled to all seven continents to photograph wildlife. He visited the Antarctic Peninsula, the Falkland Islands, and South Georgia Island to take pictures of penguins. Once he braved the rough seas to get to the isolated penguin colonies, he found the birds—especially kings—to be friendly and fascinating subjects.

Mr. Stone lives in St. Charles, Illinois, with his wife, daughter, and dog.

PHOTO ACKNOWLEDGEMENTS

All photos courtesy of Lynn M. Stone, except: © Kevin Schafer/CORBIS, p. 12 (left); © Tom Brakefield/CORBIS, p. 12 (right); © Gerald and Buff Corsi/Visuals Unlimited, pp. 15, 38 (left); © Mark Jones/Seapics.com. p. 17; © John D. Cunningham/Visuals Unlimited, p. 21; © Joe McDonald/Visuals Unlimited, p. 22; © Frank S. Todd/Danita Delmont, Agent, p. 27; © Wolfgang Kaehler, p. 33; © Fritz Pölking/Visuals Unlimited, p. 34; © Hugh Rose/Visuals Unlimited, p. 35; © North Wind Pictures, p. 40; © Robin Karpan/Visuals Unlimited, p. 42.
Map on p. 12 and diagram on p. 14 by Tim Seeley, © Lerner Publications Company.